Smart Starters

Language Arts

Motivational Exercises
to Stimulate the Brain

by Imogene Forte & Marjorie Frank

Incentive Publications
Nashville, Tennessee

Illustrated by Marta Drayton
Cover by Geoffrey Brittingham
Edited by Patience Camplair

ISBN 0-86530-643-5

1   2   3   4   5   6   7   8   9   10   08   07   06   05

PRINTED IN THE UNITED STATES OF AMERICA
www.incentivepublications.com

Table of Contents

Introduction

What is a Smart Starter?

A Smart Starter changes "extra" moments in a classroom setting into teachable moments. They are designed take short amounts of time. However, Smart Starters are NOT short on substance. The Smart Starters in this book are packed full of important skills to practice and polish or to reinforce and extend.

When are Smart Starters used?

As their name suggests, they are good for igniting learning. Instead of the slow move into a class period, lesson, or school day, a Smart Starter quick-starts the action. Each one warms up the brain with a sparkling challenge. Students also need this kind of spark at times other than the beginning of the day or class period. Use a Smart Starter any time there is a lull, or any time students need a break from a longer activity. They work effectively to stimulate thinking at the beginning, end, or middle of a class period, or any other time you can squeeze in an extra ten minutes.

Why use Smart Starters?

They're energizing! They're stimulating! They're fun! They nudge students to focus on a specific goal. They "wake-up" tired minds. They require students to make use of previously acquired knowledge and skills. Because of their short length, they give quick success and quick rewards—thus inspiring confidence and satisfaction for the learners.

How to Use This Book...

Kick-Off a New Unit

The starters are grouped by language arts strands. One or more of them might help to ease students into a new area of study. For instance, start off a unit on word meaning with *Name Two (page 10)*, or a writing unit with *Writing with a Spark (page 55)*. Or, use *Many Ways to Say It (page 76)* to introduce students to different genres of literature.

Spark a Longer Lesson

Any one of these short activities can be expanded. A starter may inspire your students to develop more questions—expanding the warm-up into a full-blown language arts lesson.

Review a Concept

Dust off those rusty skills with a Smart Starter. For instance: Have students been away from study of the grammar for a while? Refresh what they know about parts of speech with *Grammar Treasure Hunt (page 71)*. Or, strengthen their knowledge of verbals with *Shout It Out (page 76)*. Any of these Smart Starters will help to reinforce concepts previously introduced.

Charge-Up Thinking Skills & Ignite Creativity

The Smart Starters are not only for language arts class. Use them any time to stimulate minds. Doing a Smart Starter will sharpen thinking processes and challenge brains. In addition, Smart Starters work well as starting points for students to create other (similar) questions and problems.

Would You? Could You?

Put understanding of a word's meaning to work. Students can use definitions to help answer these questions. Students will need a dictionary and a partner. See how many questions they can answer in ten minutes.

1. Could you babysit with an **oaf**?

2. Would you laugh at a **quip**?

3. Could you skateboard on a **provost**?

4. Would you swim in a **morass**?

5. Could you barbeque a **query**?

6. Would you butter a **jetty**?

7. Could you **confer** with an ape?

8. Would you **boycott** a brawl?

9. Could you paint a **pirouette**?

10. Would you pet a **carnivore**?

11. Could you eat a **holograph** for lunch?

12. Would you ask a **gammon** to dance?

13. Could you put ketchup on a **cliché**?

14. Would you style hair with a **catacomb**?

15. Could you feed a melon to a **felon**?

16. Would you sit on a **sitar**?

Name Two

Have dictionaries handy as you challenge students to "name two" for each instruction you give. Read one item and wait one to two minutes while students find the word and write the answers.

1. Name two things an uncle could do with a **monocle**.
2. Name two things you should not take to a **fete**.
3. Name two ingredients found in a **nougat**.
4. Name two things you might find in a **grotto**.
5. Name two people you know who are **impetuous**.
6. Name two things you **loathe** to do.
7. Name two excuses you have **fabricated**.
8. Name two reasons why someone might wear a **snood**.
9. Name two things you might find in a **quagmire**.
10. Name two things you would like to **imbibe**.
11. Name two places you would like to **sojourn**.
12. Name two places you wouldn't want to be **vociferous**.

Don't You Dare

Here are some "don'ts" that are good advice. Students need to use their dictionaries to find out why. Give copies of the list to groups of two or three students. Find time later to let groups share their "Why Not?" explanations.

1. Don't bungee jump into an **abutment**. Why not?
2. Don't drink **brackish** water. Why not?
3. Don't try to sleep in **bedlam**. Why not?
4. Don't **jostle** a hippopotamus. Why not?
5. Don't go swimming in a **quagmire**. Why not?
6. Don't try to **hoodwink** a **pugilist**. Why not?
7. Don't paddle a boat into a **maelstrom**. Why not?
8. Don't run a marathon if you're **enervated**. Why not?
9. Don't **jeer** at your older brother's haircut. Why not?
10. Don't **thwart** a lion's attempt to eat lunch. Why not?

Where Would You Find It?

You have to know what something is in order to know where to look for it. Give each student a dictionary along with this list. Their task is to choose the correct location for each item.

1. **an aria** — in an opera — attached to a hat
2. **a pettifogger** — on a windshield — in a courtroom
3. **a coiffure** — in a beauty parlor — in a French pastry
4. **a moniker** — at a dog show — on a name tag
5. **a corona** — around the moon — behind an ear
6. **a hydrofoil** — on a river — in a spoon
7. **a clavicle** — in a salad — on a skeleton
8. **a mandrill** — on a bagel — in a zoo
9. **some kroner** — on a hamburger — in a pocket
10. **an egress** — on a leash — in a theater

Peculiar Pairs

> An **oxymoron** is a pair of words whose meanings appear to contradict each other.

Get the whole group involved in making an oxymoron mural. Hang a huge piece of mural paper along a wall. Take ten or fifteen minutes to brainstorm oxymorons.

Add more to the mural every day.

Examples:

act naturally	*industrial park*	*clearly misunderstood*
good grief	*deafening silence*	*designer jeans*
exact estimate	*working vacation*	*holy war*
freezer burn	*virtual reality*	*silent scream*
old news	*modern history*	*sanitary landfill*
small crowd	*ill health*	*unbiased opinion*

Tricky Words

Some words are easily confused with others. Each of these statements has one word that is used instead of another word whose sound is similar. Students should read the statements, find the wrong word, identify the correct word to use, and explain why the new word belongs.

1. The assurance company paid for the damage to my car.

2. We drove by the diary and bought some fresh milk.

3. The airplane was flying at an attitude of 10,000 feet.

4. We had a hard time choosing between the delicious looking deserts at the restaurant.

5. Tad had a choice of witch day to go to the dentist.

6. The car wreck left the driver in a comma.

7. I love carrots but I don't care for salary.

8. That ice cream shop doesn't except checks.

Word-A-Day

Guide your students in following these instructions to make a Word-A-Day Calendar for the upcoming week.

1. Design a fun calendar page for the week.

2. Choose seven words from the dictionary that you do not know (and that you think a classmate would not know).

3. Write one new word for each day.

4. Trade calendars with a classmate.

5. On each day of the new week, look up the new word. Learn the definition.

6. Use that word ten times during the day. You could: write it in a poem, tell it to a friend, sing it in the shower, e-mail it to someone, etc.

No Fear of the Unknown

Have fun with some unknown words. Let students choose a few of these words. Give them a moment to think about what the words *might* mean. (They should not look up their meanings.)

Each student writes a sentence that uses the words. Then, let the students find out what the words really mean. Have fun comparing the real definitions with the imagined meanings.

Example: ***My mom went from placid to placid until she was able to gather a doleful of callow watermelons.***

1. cozen	7. mediocre	13. gauche	19. macabre
2. placid	8. wraith	14. plethora	20. upbraid
3. surfeit	9. rancor	15. undulate	21. truncate
4. doleful	10. turgid	16. vacuous	22. yore
5. callow	11. savory	17. moniker	23. zenith
6. obtuse	12. sagacity	18. indelible	24. clemency

Clues to Context

Context is like a "home" for a word. It is the place a word is resting. The "resting place" gives clues to the word's meaning. Before reading each sentence aloud, read the bold word. Ask students to listen to the context of the word, consult with a partner, and write a definition for the word.

1. Weary hikers **trudged** painfully up the steep hills for hours.

2. Water just kept running out of the **porous** container.

3. How did you manage to **procure** three tickets to the sold out concert?

4. Last year, when there was a **paucity** of food at the picnic, I went home starving.

5. We were lucky that our guide was **adept** at steering our raft safely down the river.

6. The amusement park managers don't **condone** standing up on the roller coaster.

7. Stop pushing in line, or you may **instigate** a fight!

8. The **noxious** fumes from the truck made us all carsick.

Contemplate Connotation

> The **denotation** of a word is its dictionary definition.
>
> The **connotation** is all the ideas and images suggested by a word. It may be different for different readers.

The connotation of a word is much broader than the denotation. Read each denotation below. Students should identify the word, then brainstorm ideas about the word's connotation.

1. Denotation: a person or thing of great size

2. Denotation: petty and groundless rumors, usually of a personal nature

3. Denotation: a steep, sharply banked, elevated railway with small open passenger cars operated as an attraction at amusement parks and fairgrounds

4. Denotation: the science of ordering tones

5. Denotation: one who robs on the high seas

6. Denotation: a social gathering

Find the Imposter

> **Synonyms** are words that have the same or nearly the same meanings.

An imposter has shown up in each list of words. All the others synonyms of one another. Read each list aloud. Students should listen to the list and identify the imposter. Consult a dictionary if needed.

1. renovation, restitution, rectification, remuneration
2. numskull, loggerhead, savant, dullard
3. despicable, contemptible, salubrious, nefarious
4. eminent, noxious, notorious, renowned
5. unprejudiced, biased, impartial, just
6. nominal, noisome, pestilential, nocuous
7. insatiable, fastidious, rapacious, voracious
8. luminous, lustrous, gracious, brilliant
9. delirious, tedious, monotonous, dreary
10. skittish, homely, timorous, vexed

Look Out for Look Alikes

> **Homographs** are words that are spelled the same but have different meanings. They often differ in pronunciation.

Write each of the following sentences (with its clues) on a card. Give one card to each of six students. Give them one minute to find the pair of homographs that fits the sentence. After one minute, students pass their cards.

1. Why did you _____ to throw your _____ in the trash?
   (insist against) *(garbage)*

2. I _____ that you'll find the _____ hiding behind the bank.
   (surmise or guess) *(alleged culprit)*

3. Please don't _____ me in the _____.
   (abandon) *(dry wasteland)*

4. Will the lady with a _____ please take a _____?
   (fancy ribbon) *(curtsy)*

5. Scott wanted to _____ the results of the _____.
   (argue against, disagree with) *(competition)*

6. It only took a _____ to eat this _____ cream puff.
   (60 seconds) *(tiny)*

Amazing Threesomes

Each of these words has amazing possibilities. If students are clever, they can find a homophone, synonym, and antonym for each word. Give them ten minutes to try the challenge.

1. presence

2. straight

3. waste

4. stationary

5. taut

6. greater

7. some

8. won

Example: **compliment**

H: complement

S: praise

A: criticize

Dazzling Duos

Homophones are words that sound alike but have different spellings and different meanings.

Have fun creating sentences with these sound-alike pairs. Students may work in pairs to accomplish the task in ten minutes.

1. peer-pier
2. hail-hale
3. sea-see
4. cruise-crews
5. whole-hole
6. fowl-foul
7. idol-idle
8. break-brake

9. patients-patience
10. shone-shown
11. whether-weather
12. paws-pause
13. steel-steal
14. marshal-martial
15. sealing-ceiling
16. pail-pale

> *Example:*
> Put your ***clothes***
> in the drier and
> ***close*** the door.

Finish This

> An **analogy** is a relationship between two pairs of words.
> The relationship is the same in the first pair as in the second.

Set the timer for five minutes. Students can "race to the finish line" to complete the analogies. Take another five minutes to discuss how the words in each analogy are related.

1. smoke: fire *as* rain: _____

2. pebble: rock *as* _____: fish

3. _____: water *as* mitt: baseball

4. perfume: fragrant *as* _____ : fetid

5. yellow : banana *as* _____: celery

6. blush: embarrassed *as* fume: _____

7. centimeter: meter *as* inch: _____

8. evening: night *as* _____ : morning

> *Example:*
> doctor: stethescope *as* carpenter: hammer

Puzzling Pieces

Words with four or more syllables usually have become that long with the help of prefixes and suffixes. In this activity, students strengthen skills using prefixes and suffixes while they review syllabification.

Have students each draw a jigsaw puzzle on a piece of drawing paper. The puzzle should have about ten to twelve pieces. Then, give the following instructions:

1. Create a list of words that have four or more syllables.

2. Examine each word to notice the prefixes and suffixes that contribute to the word.

3. Write the words across the puzzle, making sure each word crosses into more than one puzzle piece.

4. Cut the puzzle apart. Put the pieces in an envelope.

5. Trade envelopes with a classmate and put their puzzle together.

6. Circle any prefixes or suffixes you find in the words.

Talented Roots

A **root** is the main part of the word—the part that gives the basic meaning.

Every root can be used to form different words. Brush up on the meanings of roots with this short game. Divide the group into two teams. Read one word to Team 1. The team must consult and agree on what the root is and what the root means. Then, Team 2 must name a different word with the same root. Start the next word with Team 2.

1. telegraph
2. petrify
3. astronomy
4. luminous
5. popular
6. nominate

7. pyrotechnics
8. mortal
9. marine
10. gyrate
11. invisible
12. autograph

Powerful Additions

> **Prefixes** and **suffixes** are word parts added to root words.
> A prefix is added to the beginning of a root word.
> A suffix is added to the end of a root word.

These little word parts are powerful additions because they change the meaning of a word. Work as a group to make the words described here:

Use a prefix or suffix (or both) to make a word that means......

1. capable of being reversed
2. made of gold
3. one who teaches
4. in a manner not like a friend
5. a place where bread is baked
6. one who rides a two-wheeled cycle
7. acting like a child
8. the act of a hero
9. half circle
10. one who goes on a mission
11. the middle of the night
12. not capable of being retrieved
13. one thousand watts
14. most deep
15. like magic
16. the state of being different

Compound Artistry

Show off word power and creativity with this fast-paced compound word activity. Copy this list on the board, and distribute a large piece of drawing paper to each student. Their task is think of compound words that can be made by combining two of the words. Instead of writing the word, however, they must draw an image of it. Allow the students to create as many drawings as they can in ten minutes. At the end of the alloted time, they can trade "works of art" with other students to see if they can guess the pictured compounds.

sun	sick	ways	in
fire	foot	camp	house
side	home	room	band
time	out	light	head
sea	place	some	show
down	line	day	hot
shine	town	work	ache

Time Out

Share copies of this word find with students. Ask them to circle words related to time. Words may be horizontal, vertical, or diagonal. They may also overlap.

clock	week
day	minute
noon	Monday
century	month
seasons	night
tick	tock
day	fortnight
watch	hour
night	sundial
midnight	decade
calendar	second
alarm	

g	l	k	s	e	c	o	n	d	a	y	g	h	s	g
n	t	o	u	o	q	r	c	a	l	e	n	d	a	r
o	a	l	n	p	l	o	e	g	x	s	w	q	v	h
o	d	w	d	g	m	o	n	t	h	q	a	e	n	d
n	p	a	i	f	f	k	t	e	d	k	t	a	i	g
t	y	d	a	y	z	o	u	d	c	h	c	d	g	a
a	i	c	l	h	o	u	r	m	d	b	h	n	h	z
l	a	M	o	n	d	a	y	t	s	p	x	a	t	s
c	l	o	c	k	y	p	x	w	n	q	c	f	x	q
q	a	m	l	t	d	u	m	e	o	i	q	a	m	a
r	r	p	i	p	o	r	w	e	d	t	g	j	d	q
y	m	c	j	n	b	c	e	k	s	m	g	h	s	e
i	k	w	w	u	e	k	g	r	q	a	d	t	q
p	g	d	p	n	s	t	m	i	d	n	i	g	h	t
s	e	a	s	o	n	s	e	q	g	h	a	s	x	d

The Good Word

Start this race to become the "Word Masters of the Day." Students may work in pairs to do the challenge. At the signal, students choose one of the "Good Words" from the list, recording as many forms of the word as they can. Students should continue this process with as many words as possible before the time is up.

1. generous
2. numerate
3. tolerant
4. terminate
5. celebrate
6. occupy
7. temper

8. athlete
9. friend
10. write
11. body
12. freeze
13. soft
14. mobile

Time to Rhyme

Assign students this rhyme challenge. Write as many pairs of rhyming words as you can in four minutes. Give them this scoring criteria:

1 syllable words = 1 point
(ie: fake-cake)

2 syllable words = 3 points
(ie: yellow-mellow)

3 or more syllable words = 5 points
(ie: sinister-minister)

Give the class another five minutes to write a short poem with some of their rhyming pairs.

A Book to Think About

Use some good thinking skills (from Bloom's Taxonomy of Cognitive Thinking) to review a nonfiction book that you have read. You will be practicing two things at once—using higher order thinking skills and recalling information from the book. Each student should have a nonfiction book which he or she has read recently to help them complete these three thinking tasks:

1. Knowledge: Recall three interesting facts you learned from this book. Write them down.

2. Comprehension: Summarize the purpose of the book in a short paragraph.

3. Application: Select ten key terms presented in the book. Define each one briefly. Then, classify the terms in some way.

Listen Up!

Polish up the skill of *reading for details* with this listening (or reading) exercise. Ask students to listen or read to find the answers to the questions below. Then, read the passage aloud, or give them a copy to read to themselves.

1. Where must a surfer keep the board as he or she is riding the wave?
2. At what point does the surfer stand up?
3. What is the first thing the surfer does when a good wave is coming?

When a surfer sees the perfect wave, how does she ride it? The idea is to ride along the vertical face of the wave just ahead of the wave's crest. Surfers start by kneeling or lying on the board while they wait for the right wave. When a surfer sees a good wave coming, she turns and paddles furiously toward shore, trying to move as fast as the wave. When the wave picks up the surfboard and carries it along, she stands up on the board and rides board down the vertical face of the wave. She must keep turning the board to stay ahead of the crest of the wave. If she gets it right, she can enjoy a nice ride for several minutes, moving at a good speed.

Textbook Brush-Up

Use any textbook to practice the skill of *scanning for key ideas and details.* This strengthens reading skills at the same time it sharpens understanding of content in a subject area. Supply a current textbook for each student. Assign a brief section for them to scan, or allow them to use a passage they need to read for another subject area. Give students these directions:

1. Read this section of your textbook quickly.

2. As you read, scan for the key ideas of the section.

3. After you finish, go back through the passage and record the main definitions, facts, or ideas of the passage. Write these in sequence as they appear in the passage.

4. Compare your findings with another student. See if you identified the same ideas as key ideas.

Name That Book

Here is a way to use the rich backgrounds of literature to practice comprehension skills. Students can work in small groups to collect a list of poems, fiction books, nonfiction books, or biographies they have read. Each group should recall from these sources brief comments that could help others identify the source. These might be:

memorable phrases

memorable lines

character names

one-sentence plot summaries

important facts

lesson taught

unique setting

Groups take turns writing a phrase, name, or fact on the board. The rest of the class tries to identify the book or poem and its author. See if the class can share and identify at least twenty-five of these in ten minutes.

Successful Sequencing

Use familiar stories to freshen up the skill of *sequencing*. The order of events is an important part of plot development in a story. Choose a well-known piece of literature (book, poem, or fairy tale), such as "The Three Little Pigs" or *James and the Giant Peach*. Let the group work together to complete the following outline:

Title: _____

Main Characters: _____

First Event: _____

Second Event: _____

Third Event: _____

Fourth Event: _____

Fifth Event: _____

Final Event: _____

Particular Predictions

Give every student a copy of the following comic strips and directions for this comprehension exercise.

1. Read the pictures in the first two sections of the comic strip.

2. Decide what will happen next. Draw a picture and write a "talk balloon" to show your prediction.

3. Create a new comic strip with three sections. Put pictures and words in the first two sections.

4. Trade comic strips with another student and finish the third section with predictions.

Point of Persuasion

Evaluation is a natural part of reading. Whenever you read something, you make some value judgments about how good the text is or how well it accomplishes its purpose. Challenge students to make value judgments by comparing the merits of two kinds of literature:"popular" literature and "classic" or "great" literature.

Ask students to pretend that they are judges on a committee whose task is to give a book award. The two final contestants are: J. K. Rowling's *Harry Potter and the Sorcerer's Stone* and Charles Dickens' *A Christmas Carol*.

Students should work in pairs or small groups to make a value judgment about which book should receive the book award. Each group should write its decision, along with three reasons why they chose the book.

Covers Count

We have all heard the expression, "Don't judge a book by its cover." Yet, we do make evaluations based on the covers of books. Bring several books into the classroom. Try to choose books that students may not have read. Find books with paper covers that include design and illustration.

Show the books one at a time to students. Look at all elements of the cover—front, back, and inside flaps. Ask students to brainstorm a list of evaluative words or phrases that communicate their response to the cover's effectiveness at enticing a reader to buy or read the book. Then, ask them to use that list to rate the book 1-6 (1 being the highest score). Do this with as many books as you can in the available time.

Near the end of the time, you might ask students to make their personal ranking of the books by writing the titles of the books from first to last choice.

What's the Question?

The grid below gives answers to unwritten questions about literary and comprehension terms. Students are to create a question to match each answer. They may work in pairs to write as many questions as they can in ten minutes.

1. mood
2. imagery
3. style
4. characterization
5. plot
6. sequence of events
7. point of view
8. setting

9. critique
10. protagonist
11. resolution
12. conflict
13. climax
14. flashback
15. narrator
16. parody

A Memorable Character

Spend ten or fifteen minutes focusing on a character to enhance students' skills in identifying effective characterization. Choose a recognizable character from fiction or biography. Brainstorm as a group to list as many personality traits of this character as you can remember from the story or book. Think of characteristics or events that made the character an interesting subject for reading.

When time permits, allow students to use the character traits to create one of these:

a short character sketch

a speech you might give to introduce the person

a cartoon

a short paragraph about the person

a brief anecdote about the person

Examples:

- *funny*
- *made people laugh*
- *wore crazy clothes*
- *jumped out of closets to surprise people*
- *was loyal to her friend*
- *knew weird facts*
- *stood on her head a lot*

Author Awareness

Take five minutes to make a list of as many authors as you can remember. Brainstorm this list together as a class, with one class member keeping a record of the names on the board. Then, take another five minutes to record at least two bits of information about the theme or style of each author. Ask students these questions:

What comes to mind when you hear this author's name?
What is distinctive about his or her writing?
What is the usual theme of the writing?
What style characterizes the writing?

Then, write words or phrases next to each author's name as identifying characteristics of that author's writing.

When time permits, ask students to choose one author and write a short piece in the same style or on the same theme as that author.

Listening for Devices

Review literary devices with students before sharing this list. Then, ask them to listen for literary devices in the following examples. After hearing each example, they should try to identify the device or technique the writer has used.

1. I'll be tickled pink to see you.

2. Look out for downed boughs!

3. It was so hot you could fry eggs on the sidewalk.

4. Life is a can of worms.

5. She's madder than a wet hen.

6. It's a drain on our budget to hire a plumber.

7. The toaster reaches out and grabs my toast with its flaming claws.

8. Going over Niagara Falls in a barrel was a dull way to spend the day.

9. A bird in the hand is worth two in the bush.

10. Seven snails slid stealthily.

11. Not by the hair of my chinny, chin, chin!

12. Sam seems to find the same sum.

13. My principal is like a vacuum cleaner.

14. My gum bangs, pops, sizzles, and hisses.

Reading With Style

Read this basic definition of style to students. Then, review these elements that make up the whole of an author's style:

sentence structure　　*pace*

vocabulary　　*figure of speech*

use of dialogue　　*point of view*

character development　　*tone*

word color and sound　　*time sequencing*

paragraph length and structure

> **Style** is the way an author chooses and arranges words in getting a message across or telling a story.

Read any poem by Shel Silverstein. Ask students to analyze and describe the style. Then, read a selection from any Dr. Seuss book. Ask students to analyze and describe this style, and discuss any differences they see between the two.

　　Smart Starters — Language Arts

A Personal Recommendation

Sometimes it is hard to find a good book to read. That is why a recommendation from someone else is a great gift. When you love a book, share your excitement with others. Ask students to choose a favorite fiction or nonfiction book. Have students fill out this form to make a quick recommendation to others.

Title and Author: _____

Most interesting character: _____

    because: _____

Most surprising event or situation: _____

Kind of person who would like this book: _____

Best time and place to read this book: _____

Six favorite words or phrases from the book:

_____   _____

_____   _____

_____   _____

Alphabetize Me!

Use the whole body to practice alphabetizing skills. Write each of the following words on large cards or pieces of paper. Pin each one to a student's shirt. Give the group of students three minutes to arrange themselves in alphabetical order. Try this again with the second set of words.

SET 1

1. Zeeland
2. Zambezi
3. Zimbabwe
4. zither
5. zinc
6. Zanzibar
7. Zagreb
8. ziggurat
9. Zapotec
10. zinnia
11. Zeus
12. Zola
13. zodiac
14. Zircon
15. Zeppelin
16. Zen

SET 2

1. scrawny
2. savor
3. snipe
4. staccato
5. serene
6. superb
7. stoic
8. snood
9. shrew
10. shroud
11. sacred
12. sternum
13. spend
14. savory
15. savant
16. scoundrel

Digging the Dictionary

Teams must dig into the dictionary to score in this game. Divide the group into two teams. Read each direction aloud. Teams work together to find the answer. The first team to get the answer scores a point. The first team to reach six points is the winner.

1. Find a word that has the same three beginning letters as the last name of the current president of your country.

2. Find a synonym for **horrendous**.

3. Find an antonym for **specific**.

4. Find a definition for **calculus**.

5. Find the language from which **caramel** originates.

6. Find what part of speech this word is: **glissade**.

7. Find out what you would do with a **bialy**.

8. Find a word with same first two letters as the name of your school.

9. Find a definition for **gargoyle**.

10. Find two meanings for **conflagration**.

11. Find a synonym for **brag**.

12. Name three things you might find on a **carpus**.

Hand-Drawn Definitions

Have plenty of drawing paper and dictionaries on hand for tracking down (and depicting) these definitions. Give students the following list of words. Ask them to find and draw (using no words) as many definitions as they can in the alloted time.

1. coffer
2. bassinet
3. corona
4. cygnet
5. fedora
6. polecat
7. gazette
8. minaret
9. zwieback
10. finnan haddie

11. banshee
12. flask
13. fleur de lis
14. poniard
15. fez
16. chalice
17. proboscis
18. portal
19. toupee
20. noggin

Skill: Guide Words

Words That Guide

Dictionaries and encyclopedias have helpful words at the top of each page. These words serve as a guide to what can be found on a page. Look at each page. Does the word written on the page belong there? (Write *yes* or *no*.) Then, think of another word that would be found on each page.

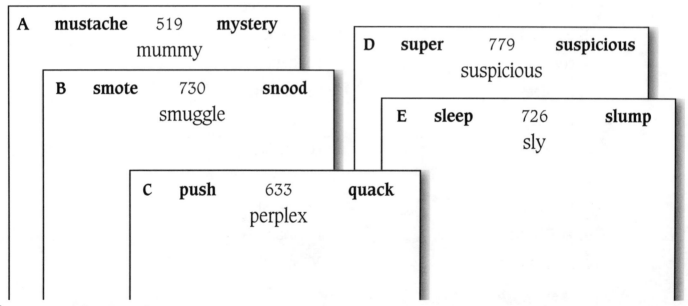

A **mustache**   519   **mystery**
mummy

B **smote**   730   **snood**
smuggle

C **push**   633   **quack**
perplex

D **super**   779   **suspicious**
suspicious

E **sleep**   726   **slump**
sly

Pair Up to Look It Up

Prepare a set of cards with research tasks such as those below. Give one question to each pair of students. Provide references such as a thesaurus, dictionary, encyclopedia, world atlas, telephone book, newspaper, almanac, or *The Guinness Book of World Records*. Set a timer for ten minutes, and send students off to track down answers.

1. What is the scientific name for the Carolina Grasshopper?
2. How far is it from Zurich, Switzerland to Chicago, Illinois?
3. Where and by whom was the first space shuttle launched?
4. List at least eight synonyms for the word joyful.
5. Who was the leader of Great Britain During World War II?
6. What is the address of the Department of Motor Vehicles in or closest to your town?
7. What is the name of the oldest living person in the world?
8. Who wrote the novel *War and Peace* ?
9. Where is the Bermuda Triangle?
10. In what city would you find the Taj Mahal?
11. What is the weather forecast for your area for tomorrow?
12. How long is the Panama Canal?

Which Reference?

Gauge students' ability to find specific information. Distribute the following list, and instruct students to find the best source for each fact.

1. the height of the world's tallest building

2. words that mean the same as **detective**

3. what books Sir Arthur Conan Doyle wrote

4. a recipe for lemon meringue pie

5. a map of the country of Borneo

6. if **rinoscerous** is spelled correctly

7. the population of the United States

8. a list of pet stores in your area

9. the major exports of Paraguay

10. what time a movie starts tonight in your town

11. the title and author of a book on extreme sports

12. which encyclopedia volume has information about space shuttles

13. how to draw a replica of your state flag

14. the history of the word **parfait**

> atlas
> almanac
> encyclopedia
> the Internet
> dictionary
> newspaper
> telephone directory
> thesaurus
> library card catalog
> library computer catalog
> recipe book
> encyclopedia index

Do You Know Dewey?

Use this quick quiz as a refresher in the Dewey Decimal System. Give the general location number for each of these book titles:

1. Grand Canyon National Park_____
2. Hotdogging and Snowboarding _____
3. Billions of Bats _____
4. Constellations for Every Kid_____
5. How Machines Work_____
6. Coping With Shyness_____
7. Speak Spanish in a Month _____
8. Gods & Spirits in Chinese Mythology_____
9. The Directory of Misinformation _____
10. Computers for Everyone _____

000-099	General Works References
100-199	Philosophy & Psychology
200-299	Religion
300-399	Social Sciences
400-499	Language
500-599	Pure Science & Mathematics
600-699	Uses of Science & Technology
700-799	Fine Arts & Sports
800-899	Literature
900-999	History, Geography & Biography

Use the News

Make use of the daily newspaper to practice information-finding skills. Supply a recent newspaper to each group of two or three students. Provide this list of questions to answer in ten minutes.

1. What is the front page headline?

2. What is the weather like?

3. How much does the paper cost?

4. What politicians or world leaders are in the news?

5. What sporting event is making news?

6. What movies are playing?

7. What are the popular cartoons?

8. What is the price range of a new pickup truck?

9. Name someone who died the week of your paper was printed.

10. Copy the headline of an article that tells some unhappy news.

It's All in the Almanac

How sharp are you with an almanac? Provide students with copies of the latest edition of an almanac. Let them work in pairs to skim the almanac for interesting information. They should write ten questions that someone could answer by using that almanac. When time permits, let the groups trade questions and find the answers in the almanac.

Examples:

Who is the most recent Olympic gold medal winner in men's figure skating?

What is the state bird of Alaska?

Which has the largest area: Bolivia, Botswana, or Bangladesh?

What are the colors in the flag of Senegal?

Who is the governor of Puerto Rico?

What is the longest single-span bridge in the world?

Words Galore

A thesaurus is an amazing collection of words—thousands of them. It supplies groups of words with similar meanings. Each pair of words below has similar meanings. Use a thesaurus to add two more similar-meaning words to each pair.

1. veritable-true _____
2. tasty-savory _____
3. brave-fearless _____
4. lovely-beautiful _____
5. scary-frightening _____
6. silly-ridiculous _____
7. boisterous-energetic _____
8. terminate-end _____
9. futile-useless _____
10. hoodwink-trick _____
11. benevolent-kind _____
12. amiable-agreeable _____

Writing With a Spark

The words authors choose add spark to their writing. Trade in words that are ordinary, general, or overused for words that are unique, specific, fresh, or colorful. Read each sentence aloud, or give students a copy of this page. The challenge is to replace each bold word or phrase with a word or phrase that has more spark.

1. It was a **dark** afternoon and the wind was blowing **hard**.

2. Pass me some of that **good** hot fudge.

3. **Huge** waves **moved** closer to the beach house.

4. The fingernails **tapping** on the window **hurt** my ears.

5. A **bright** shooting star **went** across the sky.

6. Three **big** sea lions **crawled** across the beach.

7. As the golf ball **headed** for a window, the golfer **said**, "Look out!"

8. Watch that **good** syrup **run down** over your pancakes.

Fare With Flair

At a restaurant, the words on the menu have the power to stimulate your senses and affect your choices. Guide students through this exercise to sharpen their skills with using colorful (even exotic) words.

1. Think of a name and "flavor" for a five-star restaurant. Choose the kind of food you will serve, for example: French, Asian, Indian, Greek, Italian, American, eclectic, etc.

2. Make a list of thirty words or phrases that could be used to describe your flavorful and exotic food items.

3. Create a menu for your restaurant. Use some of the words from your list as you write descriptions of at least ten menu items. Add a price to each item.

4. Trade menus with another classmate. Select items for your dinner, and calculate the price. Remember to add a generous tip!

The Missing Headlines

Use this fast-paced exercise to practice writing eye-catching titles (headlines) for news articles. Read each of these news stories aloud. Wait for two minutes after each one while students write a smashing headline for the story.

A busload of tourists claims to have seen Bigfoot on Sunday. The tour bus was headed south on Interstate 5 near Salem, Oregon, when a large creature appeared out of the woods. All 43 passengers on the bus, as well as the driver, testified to seeing the creature.

An unusual rash of spider bites has been reported in Jackson County this month. In the past four weeks, 127 bites by scorpions and other spiders have been reported. Most of the bites have occurred in the homes of victims. Normally, only 1 or 2 bites are reported each month. Local officials and scientists are searching for the causes of this increase.

A strange robbery took place Saturday night at the local sandwich shop. Juan Mirana, owner of Subs To Go, found twenty long loaves of wheat bread, a box of onions, and two large jars of pickles missing from his shop on Friday morning. There was no sign of a break-in, and the doors were still locked.

Attention-Grabbing Beginnings

The beginning of a story, article, or essay should draw the reader into the topic immediately. Since the opening sets the tone for the whole piece, it is essential that writers polish the art of grand beginnings. Read these ordinary beginnings aloud, one at a time. Students can work in pairs to replace each one with a smashing beginning.

1. Julie asked me to take care of her pet skunk.

2. The food in the school cafeteria is pretty awful.

3. There are many earthquakes in the world every day.

If time permits, the pairs of students can write a great beginning for one of these:

A. a tale about your most embarrassing moment

B. directions for how to clean your room

C. an essay convincing someone to try artichoke bubblegum

Ordinary beginning:

Middle school students protested last night at the school board meeting.

Great beginnings:

There were fireworks at the school board meeting last night.

No one could remember a school board meeting like this one.

"Down with bad school lunches!" was the cry heard at last night's school board meeting.

Places to Avoid

There are plenty of places people would rather not visit. This is a topic that can lend itself to interesting writing. Writers can name the places, but without supporting details to tell why they don't want to visit a place, the writing will be vague, dull, or incomplete.

Ask students to brainstorm a list of places they would rather not visit. Take about three minutes to do this. Then, each student should choose one of the places and write three or more details that explain why that place should be avoided.

---

sample:

Places I'd Rather Not Visit

- bottom of a crevasse
- the principal's office
- a runaway train
- basement of a haunted house
- the dentist's chair
- broken elevators
- a red ant hill
- a sinking ship
- the bottom of a bird cage

Endings With a Punch

The ending is the last thing a reader sees. It wraps up the piece of writing and leaves the reader with a final impression. Use this short activity to help students practice writing strong endings that leave a lasting impression.

Students can collaborate to create strong endings for three or more of these (as time permits).

...a poem about a musically talented gorilla

...a letter to an editor expressing a complaint

...an explanation of how to get your homework done on time

...a report of a mysterious disappearance

...a set of directions on making a perfect hot fudge sundae

...a news report about a hurricane

...a tale about a surprising event that happened at school

Idioms Galore

Review the definition of an idiom. Give students a few examples. Before reading the following short story to students, tell them to listen for idioms in the story. After reading the story, take time to let them identify the idioms they heard.

Brainstorm for a few minutes to create a list of idioms. Then, let students work in small groups to write brief stories that include several of the idioms on the list.

Losing My Cool

I was mad as a wet hen at my pain-in-the-neck brother. He burned my math book and caused me to blow my math test yesterday. I made a beeline for him to bite his head off. My anger just rolled off his back as he walked away and told me to "put a sock in it." So, I just had to hold my tongue.

Miracle Mix

Here is an exercise that will give students a chance to invent a new product and convince others to buy or use it. Read these directions to students. The task might go more quickly if students work in small groups.

1. Use your imagination to invent a "Miracle Mix." This can be a mix to eat, to bake, to spread on your skin, to put on your garden, to stir into your orange juice, or for any other purpose.

2. Write a "recipe" for the mix, listing the ingredients and directions for mixing it.

3. Create an advertisement, poster, or announcement that describes the mix, tells what it is used for, and convinces readers or listeners that they need it.

Bring Your Writing to Life

> Personification gives characteristics of living things to objects that are not alive. It is a literary device used to make writing more interesting and lively.

Students can practice adding personification to their writing. They should choose five or more of these nonliving items (as many as time permits). For each one, they can write a sentence that uses personification to make the object come alive.

Examples:

As it rises into the sky, the rock bumps its head on the clouds.

The river sings a lazy, bubbling tune to me.

Winter wind sticks out its icy tongue and frosts my nose.

my mailbox	my pillow	an ocean wave
a blender	my gym bag	snow
the shower	a lemon drop	an umbrella
a headache	the sidewalk	a science test
spaghetti	candles	
the fog	a mirror	

Metaphorically Speaking

> A **metaphor** is a comparison between two things that are not alike or are not usually in the same category.
>
> A **simile** is a metaphor that uses "like" or "as."

Students can practice speaking metaphorically by finishing each of these sentences orally. Do this as a whole group. Students can enjoy sharing different ideas about how to finish the metaphors.

> **Examples:**
> *My little brother is a tornado.*
> *Math is a hurricane of numbers.*
> *Life is a can of worms.*

1. Life is like _____ .

2. Writing a poem is like _____ .

3. Music is_____ .

4. Homework is as _____
   as _____ .

5. Losing a friend is like_____ .

6. _____ is like getting stung by a bee.

7. My temper is _____ .

8. The storm is as loud as _____ .

9. Being afraid is like _____ .

10. When _____
    is angry, it's like _____ .

Who Said That?

Dialogue adds interest and flavor to writing. This quick exercise will help students practice the use of dialogue in their writing. Copy the examples below for students. They can work in pairs to change each idea into dialogue. Encourage students to write other examples when time permits. Partners can trade sentences and turn one another's writing into direct quotations.

1. Sam asked what Bob was going to take on the camping trip. Bob answered that he would bring the tent.

2. Zac told the campers to watch out for the bear. Sam responded that there were no bears in this area.

3. Lucy ordered Suzy not to set the tent by the wasps' nest. Suzy hollered that she had no idea where the wasps' nest was.

4. The bear told Lucy that he was hungry. Lucy screamed that she didn't want to be the bear's next meal, and ran away.

Many Ways to Say It

Amaze the class with the variety of ways to write about one topic. Start by discussing any well-known tale, nursery rhyme, story, or topic. Divide the class into small groups. Assign each group a different genre in which to rewrite the story.

For example, begin with the story of "The Goose that Laid the Golden Egg." Groups can rewrite the facts of the story in these different forms:

a news article   a poem

a song   a tall tale

a limerick   a letter

an announcement   an argument

an ode   a want ad

an advertisement   a tongue twister

an explanatory essay   a thank-you note

Sentence Sleuths

declarative (D): makes a statement; tells something about a person, place, thing, or idea
interrogative (?): asks a question
imperative (I): makes a command or request and often ends with a period
exclamatory (!): communicates strong emotion or surprise

Use your best detective skills and your knowledge about sentence types to examine these sentences. Decide which kind of sentence each one is. Mark each with the symbols used above. Then, write another sentence of the same type on the same topic.

1. Look out for that shark_____

2. Did you get your spelling test back_____

3. Read the instructions on the cake mix box_____

4. My little sister is 4 years old_____

5. Please bring me a cheeseburger_____

6. I can't wait for summer vacation_____

7. Are you ready to go to soccer practice_____

8. Don't step on my pet rat_____

9. When is your birthday_____

10. My favorite team just won the World Series_____

Sentence Sense

If you don't pay close attention to your grammar, your sentences might not make sense. Read each of these sentences aloud. Lead students in a discussion about what makes the sentence "nonsensical." Help them rearrange words so that the sentence makes sense.

1. Willa enjoyed her corned beef sandwich listening to the radio.

2. We were harassed by a shark sailing our boat.

3. My sister told jokes while we were having the Johnson family for lunch.

4. The science teacher whistled to her dog driving her motorcycle.

5. I was stung by a jellyfish floating on a raft.

6. We saw the escaped chimpanzee watching television.

7. She and Sara met them and they climbed into their car.

8. Matt was distracted by the noisy neighbors doing his homework.

Lost Phrases

These prepositional phrases have lost their sentences. Without them, the phrases don't make much sense. Students can work together to create sentences that provide homes for the prepositions.

instead of an artichoke

in the goblin costume

during the hurricane

outside of the circus tent

because of the bubble gum

within the dark caverns

between the jaws of a shark

on account of her huge feet

according to the lunch menu

prior to the banana peel incident

alongside a crocodile

in spite of the cold weather

in front of the stampeding horses

underneath the front porch

No Dangling, Please!

Don't let modifiers dangle. A phrase is dangling if it is too far from the word it modifies. Write the following sentences on the board. Challenge students to find the dangling modifiers and fix them in ten minutes or less.

1. While eating its food, I suddenly noticed how fat our dog was becoming.

2. Jutting out of the sea, the swimmers were shocked to see a fin.

3. Crabs were served to the guests covered with butter.

4. Riding horseback along the beach, the ocean looked very peaceful.

5. My mother told me to put on sunscreen at least ten times this week.

6. I fixed the raft that was punctured by the shark with great care.

7. While riding my bicycle, a stray dog bit me.

8. Joe lost the music he had written by mistake.

Grammar Treasure Hunt

Here is a short adventure that will send students searching through their classroom and school for parts of speech. Each person should take a notebook, pencil, and sharp eyes as they cruise the classroom and school grounds to find and record at least three of each in fifteen minutes. Discuss and compare lists when there is time.

something that could be **a noun OR a verb** *Examples: sand, table, swing*	**adverb** describing something you saw *Example: kids moving noisily in the hall*	something that can be named with **a proper noun** *Examples: Principal, name of school*
something that can be an **object of a preposition** *Examples: basketball hoop, window*	something that can be described by **three adjectives** *Examples: flag, lunchroom, teacher*	something that can be described with a **possessive noun** *Example: the custodian's closet*

Double Duty

Some words can be used as more than one part of speech. Students can consult in pairs to show how each of these words can be used as two (or more) parts of speech. They must write or say a sentence for each use of the word.

sand	water	lecture
joke	table	spring
mint	dream	out
cold	face	time
tease	chair	break

Plurals in a Hurry

How well do students know the rules (and rule breakers) for plural nouns? This fast checkup will expose any that need more work. Read the words below, pausing briefly after each one. Students must listen to the word and write its plural form.

1. valley	13. sheep	25. great-aunt	37. radio
2. doughnut	14. hero	26. knife	38. table
3. Smith	15. leaf	27. stereo	39. piano
4. monkey	16. church	28. tablespoonful	40. mouse
5. hoof	17. child	29. tooth	41. antelope
6. buzz	18. calf	30. key	42. fairy
7. tornado	19. freezer	31. mess	43. bus
8. goose	20. cactus	32. ox	44. city
9. safe	21. echo	33. tomato	45. fly
10. cook	22. brownie	34. commander-in-chief	46. half
11. banjo	23. penny	35. porch	47. fox
12. rodeo	24. cello	36. toe	48. deer

Words That Belong

A noun becomes a possessive noun to show that something belongs to it. It's a little tricky to write nouns as possessives. Review with the class the rules on forming possessives. Then, work together to write the correct possessive for these nouns.

1. whiskers of three mice

2. the snow fort of Susie, Sam, and Stan

3. pizza of a teenager

4. the flavor of crackerjack

5. the legs of two frogs

6. the gifts that belong to both mothers-in-law

7. trunks of three elephants

8. the skateboard belonging to Jack

9. the buzzes of the bees

10. the mist of the valley

11. the eyes of the potatoes

12. feathers of the geese

13. the tail of the mouse

14. the pet jellyfish of Mr. Zax

15. the sunglasses of the lifeguards

16. the teeth of the sharks

Get Active

Active verbs are more interesting than verbs of being or linking verbs. They are more lively! There are no active verbs in these sentences. Work as a group to rewrite each sentence with an active verb.

1. That guy is bothersome.

2. He is bored most of the time.

3. He appears jittery at the amusement park.

4. He seems dazed.

5. Is he ready for the "Twister of Terror" ride?

6. After the ride, he felt dizzy.

7. He was drenched with sweat.

8. Maybe we shouldn't be angry with him.

Shout It Out

Use this oral shouting match to review verbals and strengthen understanding of each kind (gerund, participle, infinitive). Review the definition and types of "verbals." Then, show each sentence to students (on a screen or chalkboard). Students can shout out a word that is the correct kind of verbal to fill in each of the blanks.

Verbal:	a word formed from a verb, but used as a noun, adjective, or adverb
gerund:	verb form which ends in *ing* and is used as a noun
participle:	a verb form used as an adjective
infinitive:	a verb form usually introduced by to, and used as a noun, adjective, or adverb

1. _gerund_ can make your throat sore.

2. The _participle_ gorilla broke out of his cage.

3. Five firemen _participle_ ladders rushed to the scene.

4. The last one _infinitive_ the milkshake wins the prize.

5. Most of use were tired of _gerund_.

6. The _participle_ teenagers hurried to buy pizza.

7. The first one _infinitive_ to the gate will get the best seat.

8. The girls _participle_ red snow cones had red tongues.

Bad Signs

Help! These signs have some very poor usage of language. Give copies of them to students so that they can track down, explain, and fix the errors.

1.
Isn't it well that the sharks are not biting today?

2.
I can learn you to swim in one lesson!

6.
Isn't it lucky that Leroy he got away from that shark?

3.
Let's leave everyone sleep on the sand.

4.
Did you rise the flag before the sun came up?

8.
You did good to survive that dive!

5.
Don't sit your swim mask down on the sand.

9.
Not everyone can surf as good as Spike!

7.
You would of screamed too, if you had been that close to a killer whale.

10.
Did you lie your sandals on my towel?

What's Wrong?

An eavesdropper has overheard these statements. Share each one with students. The group should listen, discuss, and decide what is wrong with the usage in each sentence.

1. Don't feed nothing to the giraffes.

2. Paul he fell out of the tree house.

3. We could of had candy instead of ice cream.

4. Will these here dogs bark at us?

5. Where is the lifeguard at?

6. Anyways, I'm not going to my music lesson today.

7. How come you missed the class picnic?

8. The bear behaved bad when he ate all the berries.

9. It was a real bad idea to eat all those berries.

10. That bear sure ate a lot of berries.

Pronoun Mix-Ups

Today it is okay to use language incorrectly because the purpose is to practice getting it right. Give students this list of usage rules for pronouns. Set a timer for ten minutes. They should work in small groups to write short stories with many usage errors. When there is time, the groups can trade stories and identify and explain all of the errors.

1. A pronoun must have a clear noun to which it refers.

2. A pronoun must agree with its antecedent in person, gender, and number.

3. An indefinite pronoun used as a subject must agree with the verb.

4. The interrogative pronoun who (or whoever) is used as a subject of a sentence. Whom (or whomever) is used as an object.

5. Use subject pronouns as subjects or predicate pronouns. (Never use an object pronoun as a subject.)

6. Use object pronouns as direct objects or indirect objects. (Never use a subject pronoun as an object.)

7. In a compound subject, use subject pronouns.

8. In a compound object, use object pronouns.

Practice the Proper

Use this dictation exercise to practice proper punctuation and capitalization. Read this sample slowly and clearly. As you read, students should write the letter, punctuating and capitalizing everything correctly.

---

july 15 2005

dear aunt edna

    how are You i thought i would write and tell you about camp it has been interesting so far we are only 5 Miles from denver colorado and there is still Snow on the rocky mountains

    the food here is pretty Awful and the mosquitoes are huge we get to do fun things though like Canoeing swimming and wood carving so i guess its not too bad

    every morning the cook comes to our tent and shouts come and get it before we throw it away that is how he calls us to breakfast

    have a fun summer and ill see you when i get home

your favorite nephew
    jake

ps please send me some peanut butter jelly bread and bug repellent

---

What's That You Said?

Take turns transforming conversations into properly written quotations. Divide the class in half. One team makes a statement that tells about part of a conversation. The other team must write a sentence that includes a direct quotation. Teams take turns with each task.

Examples:

The teacher asked if anyone's homework had been eaten by dogs.
"Did anyone's dog eat their homework last night?" asked Mr. Biddle.

Ray told Mr. Biddle that his dog had eaten his homework, and wondered how his teacher knew about it.
Ray answered, "Yes, my dog ate my homework again. How did you know?"

The teacher told Ray that he saw the dog chewing on a math paper in Ray's front yard.
"Well," he said, " Your dog was making a snack of your paper while I was walking by your house!"

What's the Rule?

Put your spelling skills to the test. Share this list of twenty misspelled words. Students can work in pairs to do the following with each word:

1. Identify the rule that has been broken.
2. Write the word correctly.

Randomly call on pairs to give an explanation and correct spelling for the following words.

1. peice	8. fryed	15. lazyness
2. missunderstood	9. keies	16. hiting
3. mudy	10. ilegal	17. spraied
4. begining	11. pensil	18. ropeing
5. likeing	12. cactis	19. mosqito
6. lonly	13. magicoan	20. contaguous
7. praied	14. qeen	21. suprized

A Rule to Remember

There's one spelling rule that you can remember with a rhyme. Brush up on the ie rule, then put it to work. Read these words one at a time. After each word, students must tell:

 * whether it follows or breaks the rule
 * what part of the rule it follows

1. achieve	11. convenient	21. financier
2. quotient	12. sheik	22. retrieve
3. their	13. sleigh	23. receipt
4. piece	14. deceive	24. shriek
5. grief	15. friend	25. ceiling
6. conceit	16. hygiene	26. height
7. believe	17. freight	27. perceive
8. seize	18. vein	28. sovereign
9. either	19. science	29. heir
10. reign	20. neither	30. conceited

> **The Rule**
> Write *i* before *e*, except after *c*, or when sounding like a long *a*, as in n*ei*ghbor or w*ei*gh.

Clues to Spelling

Follow these clues and write the words correctly. Students should listen to the clues, then correctly spell the word. The first letter of the word is given.

1. precious gemstone (green)   e _____
2. book filled with synonyms   t_____
3. school for young children   k _____
4. liquid soap for your hair   s _____
5. old and valuable   a _____
6. biting insect   m_____
7. scary apparition   g _____
8. more than one person   p _____
9. the opposite of ugly   b _____
10. ten dimes   d _____
11. land surrounded by water   i_____
12. the opposite of vanilla   c _____

Spelling Turnabout

Some words can be turned around to make another word. Give students this list of words. Let them work in pairs to think of another word that can be made from the same letters. Then, they should write a clue to help someone figure out what the other word is.

1. flea	7. night	
2. cures	8. mental	
3. heart	9. cheat	
4. listen	10. march	
5. trainer	11. alert	
6. dread	12. rages	

Example:

word	diary
clue	where cows are milked
new word	dairy

Weird and Wacky Words

Here are some words that push spelling skills to the limit. They are strangely spelled or unusual words. Give the list below to students. *(Some of the words are spelled correctly, and some are not.)* Provide dictionaries, as well. Give them ten or fifteen minutes to track down correct spellings. Students can work in groups of two or three.

1. rogue
2. ogre
3. dungun
4. jodpurs
5. menagerie
6. hyperbole
7. catastrofe
8. elixir
9. morgue
10. tongue

11. surgun
12. et cetera
13. petit fours
14. anacronism
15. incisors
16. bamboozle
17. onomatopoeia
18. etiqette
19. cipher
20. sousaphone

Warning!

| PAY ATTENSHUN! |
| DO NOT FEED THE AMINALS |

| School is canseled! |

| Nashunal Emergancy! |

Show students these warning signs.

Ask them to identify the spelling errors.

Ask each student to make two more warning signs. Each one should include one or more misspellings of commonly used words.

When the signs are finished, number them and post them around the room. Each student should visit every sign to identify misspelled words. Ask them to record the correct spelling for those words.

After the Test

Here is a way to test spelling without giving a test. The test has already been taken! Distribute a copy of this finished test to each student. They should search for misspelled words, score the test, and give correct spellings.

Spelling Test	*Julie*
1. eazy	11. paradice
2. majic	12. dimond
3. meant	13. lawyer
4. dinosar	14. excagerate
5. grammer	15. elephent
6. balloon	16. calender
7. morgage	17. jooce
8. jurney	18. iceicle
9. noughty	19. jealous
10. breckfast	20. carecter

Answers

PAGE 9

Some answers will vary.
1. maybe
2. probably
3. no
4. probably not
5. no
6. no
7. possibly
8. probably
9. yes
10. yes
11. no
12. no
13. no
14. no
15. yes
16. probably not

PAGE 10

Answers will vary. Give credit for anything that makes sense with the meaning of the word.

PAGE 11

Explanations will vary.
1. An abutment would be hard.
2. Brackish water is unclean.
3. Bedlam is not restful.
4. Bumping into a hippo could be dangerous.
5. A quagmire, or swamp, is dangerous for swimming.
6. Deceiving a professional boxer could get you beaten up!
7. A whirlpool could sink you.
8. You are too weak to run.
9. Your brother might get mad at you for laughing at him.
10. The lion may eat you!

PAGE 12

1. opera
2. courtroom
3. beauty parlor
4. name tag
5. moon
6. river
7. skeleton
8. zoo
9. pocket
10. theater

PAGE 13

Answers will vary.

PAGE 14

1. wrong word: **assurance**; right word: **insurance**
2. wrong word: **diary**; right word: **dairy**
3. wrong word: **attitude**; right word: **altitude**
4. wrong word: **deserts**; right word: **desserts**
5. wrong word: **witch**; right word: **which**
6. wrong word: **comma**; right word: **coma**
7. wrong word: **salary**; right word: **celery**
8. wrong word: **except**; right word: **accept**

PAGE 15

Calendars will vary.

PAGE 16

Definitions:
1. cozen—deceive
2. placid—tranquil
3. surfeit—excess
4. doleful—sad
5. callow—immature
6. obtuse—blunt
7. mediocre—average, ordinary
8. wraith—a ghost
9. rancor—deep spite or malice
10. turgid—swollen
11. savory—tasty
12. sagacity—wisdom
13. gauche—lacking grace
14. plethora—excess
15. undulate—move in waves
16. vacuous—empty
17. moniker—nickname
18. indelible—permanent
19. macabre—gruesome
20. upbraid—to rebuke harshly
21. truncate—to shorten by cutting
22. yore—a time long ago
23. zenith—highest point
24. clemency—forgiveness

PAGE 17

Definitions:
1. trudged—walked heavily and slowly
2. porous—full of pores or holes
3. procure—obtain, get
4. paucity—smallness of quantity
5. adept—skilled
6. condone—overlook
7. instigate—start
8. noxious—poisonous

Answers

PAGE 18
Ideas will vary. Some connotations might include the following.
1. giant—a huge, frightening hairy creature that looks strange and threatens people
2. gossip—juicy secrets and harmful stories whispered behind someone's back
3. roller coaster—a wild, terrifying amusement park ride that makes passengers scream
4. music—wonderful, colorful, and pleasing rhythmic sounds for dancing
5. pirate—a colorful, dangerous character with a wooden leg, parrot, and eye patch
6. party—a fun gathering with lots of good food, games, and dancing

PAGE 19
1. remunerations
2. savant
3. salubrious
4. noxious
5. biased
6. nominal
7. fastidious
8. gracious
9. delirious
10. homely

PAGE 20
1. refuse
2. suspect
3. desert
4. bow
5. contest
6. minute

PAGE 21
Homophones below. Synonyms and antonyms will vary.
1. presence—presents
2. straight—strait
3. waste—waist
4. stationary—stationery
5. taut—taught
6. greater—grater
7. some—sum
8. won—one

PAGE 22
Sentences will vary.

PAGE 23
Answers may vary. Some possibilities are:
1. storm
2. minnow
3. bucket or pail
4. garbage
5. green
6. angry
7. yard
8. dawn

PAGE 24
Puzzles will vary.

PAGE 25
Roots, meanings, and other possible words:
1. tele—far
   telephone
2. petr—stone
   petroleum
3. astr—star
   astronaut
4. lum—light
   illuminate
5. pop—people
   population
6. nom—name
   misnomer
7. pyro—fire
   pyromaniac
8. mort—death
   mortality
9. mar—sea
   maritime
10. gyr—whirl
    gyroscope
11. vis—see
    visibility
12. graph—write
    graphic

PAGE 26
1. reversible
2. golden
3. teacher
4. unfriendly
5. bakery
6. bicyclist
7. childish
8. heroism
9. semicircle
10. missionary
11. midnight
12. irretrievable
13. kilowatt
14. deepest
15. magical
16. difference

PAGE 27
Answers will vary.

PAGE 28
Check puzzles to see that several of the "time" words are circled.

PAGE 29
Answers will vary.
Example: occupy, occupancy, occupied, occupies, occupant
Example: temper, tempers, tempered, tempering, intemperate

PAGE 30
Answers will vary.

PAGE 31
Answers will vary.

PAGE 32
1. ahead of the wave's crest
2. as soon as the wave picks up the board and begins to carry it along

3. turns the board and paddles towards shore, trying to move as fast as the wave

PAGE 33
Answers will vary.

PAGE 34
Answers will vary.

PAGE 35
Outlines will vary.

PAGE 36
Cartoons will vary.

PAGE 37
Answers will vary.

PAGE 38
Answers will vary.

PAGE 39
Question will vary. Definitions follow.
1. **mood:** the feeling or atmosphere created by the writer
2. **imagery:** the use of images in a passage

3. **style:** the way an author chooses and arranges words in getting a message across or telling a story
4. **characterization:** the act of creating or describing a character in a written work
5. **plot:** series of events that make up a story
6. **sequence of events:** the order in which things happen in a story
7. **point of view:** the perspective from which a story is told
8. **setting:** the time and place of a story
9. **critique:** a review of a story
10. **protagonist:** the main character in a story, usually one who faces a problem or conflict

11. **resolution:** the ending or solving of the conflict in a story, play, or poem-story
12. **conflict:** a problem or struggle between two people, things, or ideas in a piece of literature
13. **climax:** the highest point of suspense in a written work
14. **flashback:** part of a story, play, or story-poem that tells about events which happened earlier than the current setting of the story
15. **narrator:** the person telling the story
16. **parody:** a work that makes fun of another work by imitating some aspect of the other writer's style

PAGE 40
Answers will vary.

PAGE 41
Answers will vary.

PAGE 42
1. idiom
2. assonance
3. hyperbole
4. metaphor
5. cliché or idiom
6. pun
7. personification
8. understatement
9. proverb
10. alliteration
11. rhythm
12. consonance
13. simile
14. onomatopoeia

PAGE 43
Answers will vary.

PAGE 44
Recommendations will vary.

PAGE 45
List 1
1. Zagreb
2. Zambezi

3. Zanzibar
4. Zapotec
5. Zeeland
6. Zen
7. Zeppelin
8. Zeus
9. ziggurat
10. Zimbabwe
11. zinc
12. zinnia
13. Zircon
14. zither
15. zodiac
16. Zola

List 2
1. sacred
2. savant
3. savor
4. savory
5. scoundrel
6. scrawny
7. serene
8. shrew
9. shroud
10. snipe
11. snood
12. spend
13. staccato
14. sternum

Answers

15. stoic
16. superb

PAGE 46

1. Answers will vary.
2. Some possible answers: horrible, dreadful, awful, etc.
3. Some possible answers: vague, ambiguous
4. a method of mathematical computation
5. Spanish
6. noun or verb
7. eat it
8. Answers will vary.
9. a grotesquely carved figure, sometimes on a building
10. fire or war
11. Possible answer: boast
12. Anything you would find on a wrist: watch, bracelet, or freckle

PAGE 47

Pictures should illustrate these definitions:

1. coffer—a chest for holding money
2. bassinet—a baby's basket-like bed
3. corona—a ring of light or halo
4. cygnet—a baby swan
5. fedora—a hat with a creased crown
6. polecat—a skunk
7. gazette—a newspaper
8. minaret—a tower
9. zwieback—a piece of toast
10. finnan haddie—a fish
11. banshee—a ghostly figure
12. flask—a container for liquid, usually small, flat, with a narrow outlet
13. fleur de lis—iris, or a stylized iris figure
14. poniard—a dagger

15. fez—a cone shaped, flat top hat with a tassel
16. chalice—a cup or bowl with a stem
17. proboscis—a nose or snout
18. portal—a gate or doorway
19. toupee—a wig
20. noggin—a small mug or wooden cup OR a head

PAGE 48

A no
B yes
C no
D yes
E no
   Check student words for appropriateness.

PAGE 49

1. Dissosteira carolina
2. Answers will vary slightly but should be around 4,400 miles.
3. Kennedy Space Center in Florida,

United States (NASA)
4. Answers will vary, may include: happy, ecstatic, glad, gay, delighted, felicitous, blissful, enjoyable, pleasant, etc.
5. Winston Churchill
6. Answers will vary.
7. Answers will vary.
8. Leo Tolstoy
9. western Atlantic Ocean, off the coast of Florida
10. Agra, India
11. Answers will vary.
12. 80 kilometers

PAGE 50

Answers may vary. "The Internet" is a possible answer for most of the items. The following are other possible answers.

1. almanac; encyclopedia
2. thesaurus; dictionary
3. library card catalog,

library computer catalog, encyclopedia
4. recipe book
5. atlas; encyclopedia
6. dictionary
7. almanac; atlas
8. telephone directory

9. atlas; encyclopedia; almanac
10. newspaper
11. library card or computer catalog
12. encyclopedia index
13. encyclopedia
14. dictionary

PAGE 51

1. 900–999
2. 700–799
3. 500–599
4. 500–599
5. 600–699
6. 100–199
7. 400–499
8. 200–299
9. 000–099
10. 600–699

PAGE 52
Answers will vary.
PAGE 53
Questions will vary.
PAGE 54
Answers will vary.
PAGE 55
Answers will vary.
PAGE 56
Answers will vary.
PAGE 57
Headlines will vary.
PAGE 58
Answers will vary.
PAGE 59
Answers will vary.
PAGE 60
Answers will vary.
PAGE 61
Answers will vary.
PAGE 62
Answers will vary.
PAGE 63
Answers will vary.

PAGE 64
Answers will vary.
PAGE 65
Answers may vary somewhat in construction or sequence of phrases.
Note: The correct way to write dialogue is to begin a new paragraph each time someone new speaks.
1. Sam asked Bob, "What are you going to take on the camping trip?" Bob answered, "I will bring the tent."
2. "Watch out for the bear!" Zac told the campers. "There are no bears in this area," responded Sam.
3. "Don't set the tent by the wasps' nest, Suzy," ordered Lucy. Suzy hollered, "I

have no idea where the wasps' nest is!"
4. "I'm hungry," the bear told Lucy. "I don't want to be your next meal!" screamed Lucy as she ran away.

PAGE 66
Answers will vary.
PAGE 67
Answers may vary.
1. !
2. ?
3. I
4. D
5. I
6. D or !
7. ?
8. I or !
9. ?
10. ! or D
PAGE 68
Answers will vary.
PAGE 69
Answers will vary.

PAGE 70
Answers may vary. These are possible answers:
1. While our dog was eating its food, I suddenly noticed how fat he was becoming.
2. The swimmers were shocked to see a fin jutting out of the sea.
3. Crabs covered with butter were served to the guests.
4. The ocean looked very peaceful as I was horseback riding on the beach.
5. My mother told me at least ten times this week to put on sunscreen.
6. I fixed with great care the raft that was punctured by the shark.
7. A stray dog bit me while I was riding

on my bicycle.
8. Joe lost, by mistake, the music he had written.

PAGE 71
Answers will vary.
PAGE 72
Answers will vary.
PAGE 73
1. valleys
2. doughnuts
3. Smiths
4. monkeys
5. hooves or hoofs
6. buzzes
7. tornadoes
8. geese
9. safes
10. cooks
11. banjos
12. rodeos
13. sheep
14. heroes
15. leaves
16. churches
17. children
18. calves

Answers

19. freezers
20. cacti
21. echoes
22. brownies
23. pennies
24. cellos
25. great-aunts
26. knives
27. stereos
28. tablespoonfuls
29. teeth
30. keys
31. messes
32. oxen
33. tomatoes
34. commanders-in-chief
35. porches
36. toes
37. radios
38. tables
39. pianos
40. mice
41. antelope
42. fairies
43. buses
44. cities
45. flies
46. halves
47. foxes
48. deer

PAGE 74
1. mice's whiskers
2. Susie, Sam, and Stan's snow fort
3. teenager's pizza
4. crackerjack's flavor
5. frogs' legs
6. mothers-in-law's gifts
7. elephants' trunks
8. Jack's skateboard
9. bees' buzzes
10. valley's mist
11. potatoes' eyes
12. geese's feathers
13. the mouse's tail
14. Mr. Zax's jellyfish
15. the lifeguards' sunglasses
16. sharks' teeth

PAGE 75
Answers will vary.

PAGE 76
Answers will vary.

PAGE 77
1. good instead of well
2. teach instead of learn
3. let instead of leave
4. raise instead of rise
5. set instead of sit
6. cross out he
7. have instead of of
8. well instead of good
9. well instead of good
10. lay instead of lie

PAGE 78
1. double negative—*anything* instead of *nothing*
2. double subject—drop *he* or *Paul*
3. use of *of* with would, could, should—use have instead of *of*
4. don't use *here* with demonstrative pronoun—drop *here*
5. don't use *at* after where—drop *at*
6. no such word as *anyways*—drop the *s* at the end
7. use *why* instead of *how come*
8. *bad* is an adjective, *badly* is an adverb—use *badly* instead of *bad* in this sentence
9. *real* is an adjective, *really* is an adverb—use *really* instead of *real* in this sentence.
10. *sure* is an adjective, *surely* is an adverb—use *surely* instead of *sure* in this sentence.

PAGE 79
Answers will vary.

PAGE 80
Answers may vary slightly.

July 15, 2005
Dear Aunt Edna,
How are you? I thought I would write and tell you about camp. It has been interesting so far. We are only 5 miles from Denver, Colorado and there is still snow on the Rocky Mountains. The food is pretty awful and the mosquitoes are huge! We get to do fun things, though, like canoeing, swimming, and wood carving, so I guess it's not too bad. Every morning the cook comes to our tent and shouts, "Come and get it before we throw it away!" That is how he calls us to breakfast. Have a fun summer and I'll see you when I get home.
Your favorite nephew,
Jake
P.S. Please send me some peanut butter, jelly, bread, and bug repellent.

PAGE 81
Answers will vary.

PAGE 82
1. piece
2. misunderstood
3. muddy
4. beginning
5. liking
6. lonely
7. prayed
8. fried

9. keys
10. illegal
11. pencil
12. cactus
13. magician
14. queen
15. laziness
16. hitting
17. sprayed
18. roping
19. mosquito
20. contagious
21. surprised

PAGE 83
1. follows i before e except after c
2. follows i before e except after c
3. rule breaker
4. follows i before e except after c
5. follows i before e except after c
6. follows i before e except after c
7. follows i before e except after c
8. rule breaker
9. rule breaker

10. follows when sounding like long a
11. follows i before e except after c
12. rule breaker
13. follows when sounding like long a
14. follows i before e except after c
15. follows i before e except after c
16. follows i before e except after c
17. follows when sounding like long a
18. follows when sounding like long a
19. rule breaker
20. rule breaker
21. rule breaker
22. follows i before e except after c
23. follows i before e except after c
24. follows i before e except after c

25. follows i before e except after c
26. rule breaker
27. follows i before e except after c
28. rule breaker
29. rule breaker
30. follows i before e except after c

PAGE 84
1. emerald
2. thesaurus
3. kindergarten
4. shampoo
5. antique
6. mosquito
7. ghost
8. people
9. beautiful or beauty
10. dollar
11. island
12. chocolate

PAGE 85
Answers may vary. Some possible answers are:
1. leaf
2. curse
3. earth

4. silent
5. terrain
6. dared
7. thing
8. lament
9. teach
10. charm
11. alter
12. gears

PAGE 86
All words are spelled correctly except for those below:
3. dungeon
4. jodhpurs
7. catastrophe
11. surgeon
14. anachronism
18. etiquette

PAGE 87
Correct spelling of examples:
" Pay Attention!"
" Do Not Feed the Animals";
" School is Canceled";
" National Emergency"
Student signs will vary.

PAGE 88
1. easy
2. magic
3. meant (correct)
4. dinosaur
5. grammar
6. balloon (correct)
7. mortgage
8. journey
9. naughty
10. breakfast
11. paradise
12. diamond
13. lawyer (correct)
14. exaggerate
15. elephant
16. calendar
17. juice
18. icicle
19. jealous (correct)
20. character